# Dunbar

by Iain Gray

79 Main Street, Newtongrange,
Midlothian EH22 4NA
Tel: 0131 344 0414   Fax: 0845 075 6085
E-mail: info@lang-syne.co.uk
www.langsyneshop.co.uk

Design by Dorothy Meikle
Printed by Printwell Ltd
© Lang Syne Publishers Ltd 2022

All rights reserved. No part of this publication may be reproduced, stored or introduced into a retrieval system, or transmitted in any form or by any means (electronic, mechanical, photocopying, recording or otherwise) without the prior written permission of Lang Syne Publishers Ltd.

ISBN 978-1-85217-757-7

# Dunbar

**MOTTO:**
In readiness

**CREST:**
A horse's head, reined and bridled

**TERRITORIES:**
East Lothian, Wigtownshire,
the Borders, Morayshire

**NAME** variations include:
  Dounbar
  Dounber
  Dumbare
  Dunbarr

*Chapter one:*

# The origins of popular surnames

by George Forbes and Iain Gray

***If you don't know where you came from, you won't know where you're going*** **is a frequently quoted observation and one that has a particular resonance today when there has been a marked upsurge in interest in genealogy, with increasing numbers of people curious to trace their family roots.**

Main sources for genealogical research include census returns and official records of births, marriages and deaths – and the key to unlocking the detail they contain is obviously a family surname, one that has been 'inherited' and passed from generation to generation.

No matter our station in life, we all have a surname – but it was not until about the middle of the fourteenth century that the practice of being identified by a particular surname became commonly established throughout the British Isles.

Previous to this, it was normal for a person to be identified through the use of only a forename.

But as population gradually increased and there were many more people with the same forename, surnames were adopted to distinguish one person, or community, from another.

Many common English surnames are patronymic in origin, meaning they stem from the forename of one's father – with 'Johnson,' for example, indicating 'son of John.'

It was the Normans, in the wake of their eleventh century conquest of Anglo-Saxon England, a pivotal moment in the nation's history, who first brought surnames into usage – although it was a gradual process.

For the Normans, these were names initially based on the title of their estates, local villages and chateaux in France to distinguish and identify these landholdings.

Such grand descriptions also helped enhance the prestige of these warlords and generally glorify their lofty positions high above the humble serfs slaving away below in the pecking order who had only single names, often with Biblical connotations as in Pierre and Jacques.

The only descriptive distinctions among the peasantry concerned their occupations, like 'Pierre the swineherd' or 'Jacques the ferryman.'

Roots of surnames that came into usage in England not only included Norman-French, but also Old French, Old Norse, Old English, Middle English, German, Latin, Greek, Hebrew and the Gaelic languages of the Celts.

The Normans themselves were originally Vikings, or 'Northmen', who raided, colonised and eventually settled down around the French coastline.

They had sailed up the Seine in their longboats in 900AD under their ferocious leader Rollo and ruled the roost in north eastern France before sailing over to conquer England in 1066 under Duke William of Normandy – better known to posterity as William the Conqueror, or King William I of England.

Granted lands in the newly-conquered England, some of their descendants later acquired territories in Wales, Scotland and Ireland – taking not only their own surnames, but also the practice of adopting a surname, with them.

But it was in England where Norman rule and custom first impacted, particularly in relation to the adoption of surnames.

This is reflected in the famous *Domesday Book*, a massive survey of much of England and Wales, ordered by William I, to determine who owned what, what it was worth and therefore how much they were liable to pay in taxes to the voracious Royal Exchequer.

Completed in 1086 and now held in the National Archives in Kew, London, 'Domesday' was an Old English word meaning 'Day of Judgement.'

This was because, in the words of one contemporary chronicler, "its decisions, like those of the Last Judgement, are unalterable."

It had been a requirement of all those English landholders – from the richest to the poorest – that they identify themselves for the purposes of the survey and for future reference by means of a surname.

This is why the *Domesday Book*, although written in Latin as was the practice for several centuries with both civic and ecclesiastical records, is an invaluable source for the early appearance of a wide range of English surnames.

Several of these names were coined in connection with occupations.

These include Baker and Smith, while Cooks, Chamberlains, Constables and Porters were to be found carrying out duties in large medieval households.

The church's influence can be found in names such as Bishop, Friar and Monk while the popular name of Bennett derives from the late fifth to mid-sixth century Saint Benedict, founder of the Benedictine order of monks.

The early medical profession is represented by Barber, while businessmen produced names that include Merchant and Sellers.

Down at the village watermill, the names that cropped up included Millar/Miller, Walker and Fuller, while other self-explanatory trades included Cooper, Tailor, Mason and Wright.

Even the scenery was utilised as in Moor, Hill, Wood and Forrest – while the hunt and the chase supplied names that include Hunter, Falconer, Fowler and Fox.

Colours are also a source of popular surnames, as in Black, Brown, Gray/Grey, Green and White, and would have denoted the colour of the clothing the person habitually wore or, apart from the obvious exception of 'Green', one's hair colouring or even complexion.

The surname Red developed into Reid, while

Blue was rare and no-one wanted to be associated with yellow.

Rather self-important individuals took surnames that include Goodman and Wiseman, while physical attributes crept into surnames such as Small and Little.

Many families proudly boast the heraldic device known as a Coat of Arms, as featured on our front cover.

The central motif of the Coat of Arms would originally have been what was sometimes borne on the shield of a warrior to distinguish himself from others on the battlefield.

Not featured on the Coat of Arms, but highlighted on page three, are the family motto and related crest – with the latter frequently different from the central motif.

Adding further variety to the rich cultural heritage that is represented by surnames is the appearance in recent times in lists of the most common names found throughout the United Kingdom of ones that include Khan, Patel and Singh – names that have proud roots in the vast sub-continent of India.

Echoes of a far distant past can still be found in our surnames and they can be borne with pride in commemoration of our forebears.

*Chapter two:*

# Battlefields and sieges

**A locational, or habitational, surname, 'Dunbar' features prominently in the historical record not only through the Scottish southeast coastal town of the name but also thanks to those who have borne it, in a variety of spelling variations, over the centuries.**

Dunbar itself, of course, had been existence for many centuries before the arrival of those who would adopt it as their name.

Located in East Lothian, about 30 miles (48km) east of Edinburgh and only the same approximate distance from the border with England, its name derives from the Gaelic dùn barra, meaning 'summit fort' which, in turn, derives from the Cumbric dialect of what was formerly Northumbria, now Northumberland, in the north of England.

In its Cumbric form, 'Dunbar' is din-bar, also meaning 'summit fort' – a strategic stronghold set atop a hill dominating the landscape – and traces of such an iron age fortification have been found by archaeologists.

Occupied by the tribe known as the Votadini, it was held for a time by the Romans while, during the sixth century, it became part of the powerful Anglian kingdom of Northumbria.

Subjected to warfare over the centuries, it was not until 1018, following King Malcolm II's victory over the Northumbrians at the battle of Carham, that it was finally absorbed into the kingdom of Scotland.

Those who would come to bear the Dunbar name were originally settled in Northumbria, but one theory is that they may have traced a descent from Crìnàn of Dunkeld, in Perthshire, whose date of birth is not known but he is believed to have died in 1045.

Hereditary abbot of the monastery of Dunkeld and married to a daughter of Malcolm II, his eldest son reigned in Scotland from 1034 to 1040 as King Duncan I, while a second son, Maldred, was the father of Gospatrick, Earl of Northumbria.

It is this figure – also known as 'Cospatrick', meaning 'servant of St Patrick' – who was the first of those who would take the Dunbar name after settling there in about 1072 during the reign of King Malcolm III.

Also known as Gospatrick I, he died in about 1073, and his descendants came to hold the title of

Earl of Lothian, or Earl of Dunbar – with the Dunbar earldom also later known as the Earldom of March.

The first in the line of succession from Gospatrick I was his son Gospatrick II. He died in about 1138 and was succeeded by his son Gospatrick III, who inherited territories in East Lothian, the Scottish Borders and in the family's original seat of Northumbria.

Deeply religious, he gifted many of his lands to the Church and, before his death in 1166, became a monk.

He fathered two sons, Sir Patrick de Greenlaw – ancestor of the Earls of Home today and one of whose most famous sons was Sir Alec-Douglas Home, Baron Home of the Hirsel, who served as British Prime Minister from 1963 to 1964 – and Waltheof, Earl of Lothian.

Waltheof's eldest son, Patrick I, Earl of Dunbar, was the first of the line to hold important royal positions – a sign of the trust in which the family was held – including the witnessing of royal charters and travelling in the entourage of both King William I, better known as William the Lyon, and Alexander III on diplomatic missions south of the border.

He also made an important marriage, to Ada, an illegitimate daughter of William the Lyon.

He died in 1232 and his eldest son, Patrick II, born in 1185 and who died in 1249, was one of the Scottish nobles who donned his battle armour to help quell a rebellion against the Crown by the Thane of Argyll.

His son Patrick IV, 8th Earl of March, described himself as 'of Dunbar' – and was accordingly known as 'Patrick de (of) Dunbar.'

Along with nobles who included Robert Bruce, 5th Lord of Annandale and grandfather of the future warrior king Robert the Bruce, he was one of the competitors for the throne of Scotland in 1291.

This had followed the death of King Alexander III in a riding accident during a storm in 1286 and the subsequent death four years later of his sole heir to the throne, Margaret, Maid of Norway.

Dunbar's claim to the throne was based on the fact that his great-grandmother Ada, Countess of Dunbar, had been an illegitimate daughter of William the Lyon.

But both Dunbar and Bruce were unsuccessful in their claim and, in a judgement that had been 'arbitrated' by the ambitious King Edward I of

England – known as the 'Hammer of the Scots' – the claimant John Baliol was declared the rightful heir.

Dunbar died in 1308 and was succeeded by his son Patrick of Dunbar, 9th Earl of March who, following the decisive defeat of King Edward II's army at the battle of Bannockburn in 1314, had granted the English king sanctuary for a time in Dunbar Castle as he fled to safety.

But he later became reconciled to Bruce, taking up arms in Scotland's cause during the Second War of Independence and was also one of the signatories to the famous appeal to the Pope in 1320 for recognition of Scotland's right to freedom and independence, the Declaration of Arbroath.

In October of 1346, he was in command of the right wing of the Scottish army at the battle of Neville's Cross, west of Durham, when a 12,000-strong Scottish force led by King David II was soundly defeated by an English army roughly half that strength.

Patrick of Dunbar escaped from the battlefield where, among the many dead, lay the body of John Randolph, 3rd Earl of Moray, brother of his wife Agnes Randolph, Countess of Dunbar and March and better known to posterity as the feisty 'Black Agnes'.

The daughter of Thomas Randolph, Earl of Moray and Isabel Stewart, she married Patrick de Dunbar in 1324, becoming his second wife.

*Black Agnes at the siege of Dunbar Castle*

Known as Black Agnes because of her dark complexion, in 1338, eight years before the disastrous battle of Neville's Cross, she was left in charge of Dunbar Castle while her husband was engaged in other pressing military matters.

On September 15 of that year, the stronghold came under siege by an English army commanded by William Montague, 1st Earl of Salisbury.

With her husband away, Montague could well have been forgiven for thinking the castle would easily fall – but Black Agnes was no frail pushover – and the siege was destined to last five long months before he gave up in despair.

Surrounded by up to 20,000 besiegers and asked to surrender, Agnes is nevertheless said to have declared: "Of Scotland's king I haud my house, and pay him meat and fee, and I will keep my gude auld house, while my house will keep me."

The earl's first ploy to weaken the castle's defences was to catapult immense rocks against its ramparts, but Black Agnes merely scoffed at this, having one of her maids disdainfully dust off the ramparts with a handkerchief.

Undeterred, the earl then put a huge siege engine known as a sow into action – to which Agnes reacted by heaving one of the large boulders that, ironically had previously been thrown at the ramparts, onto the sow and crushing it.

An increasingly frustrated Montague then bribed the guard of one of the castle's entrances with money to unlock the gate at a pre-determined time, so he and his men could make a surprise entry.

The canny guard duly pocketed the bribe – only to then inform Agnes.

Forewarned, she set a trap by ordering the gate opened just before the earl and a band of his men charged forward – the earl only narrowly escaping as the Scots lowered the portcullis, hoping to separate him from his men.

As he fled back to his encampment with his tail between his legs, Agnes taunted him: "Farewell, Montague, I intended that you should have supped with us, and assisted us in defending the castle against the English."

Meanwhile Agnes's brother John Randolph, 3rd Earl of Moray and who was destined to lose his life eight years later at the battle of Neville's Cross, had earlier been captured by the English and taken to the earl's encampment.

Ordering a rope placed around his neck, the

earl warned Agnes he would hang him if she did not surrender the castle.

But if he thought this would sway her, he was sadly mistaken. She is said to have replied – tongue in cheek, it is to be hoped – that, in effect, it would actually be to her benefit if her brother was hanged, because she would inherit his earldom.

A tongue in cheek remark or not, the earl withdrew the threat and decided to starve the castle into submission by blockading all access by road – but he had forgotten about access from the sea.

To relieve the castle, Ramsay of Dalhousie led a force of 40 men from Edinburgh to Dunbar and, commandeering boats, approached the castle from the sea and entered by a rear gate.

Wasting no time, they charged out of the castle and scattered the earl's surprised guard, chasing them all the way back to their encampment.

The earl finally accepted defeat and lifted the siege on June 10 – with one ballad relating his final words to Agnes before departing were: "Cam (came) I early, cam I late, I found Agnes at the gate.'

The redoubtable Black Agnes died just over 30 years later, only a few short months before her husband Patrick of Dunbar.

*Chapter three:*

# Decline and fall

**Described as 'one of the most powerful nobles in Scotland of his time', the grandly-titled George of Dunbar, 10th Earl of Dunbar and March, 12th Lord of Annandale and Lord of the Isle of Man, born in 1340, took to his battle armour in what was proving to be interminable war with England.**

In August of 1388 he was among the estimated 2,900 Scots commanded by James Douglas, 2nd Earl of Douglas, on the field of battle at Otterburn, Northumbria after Douglas had raided into England.

With George of Dunbar's kinsman John Dunbar, Earl of Moray, commanding the Scottish right wing and Douglas the left, they met a 3,900 strong English army commanded by Henry 'Hotspur' Percy.

Douglas was killed, but the Scots proved victorious and Hotspur was captured – inspiring the ballads *The Battle of Chevy Chase* and *The Battle of Otterburn* – while Dunbar took responsibility for leading the Scots back over the border.

Destined not to live through peaceful times

for at least another few centuries, George Dunbar, 11th Earl of Dunbar and March, was the last of the family to hold the titles, after falling foul of King James I – despite having attended his coronation at Scone and being knighted by him.

Born in about 1370, in 1425 he, along with the Earl of Douglas, Earl of Lennox, Duke of Albany and other nobles, was imprisoned on the orders of the king on charges of corruption in Scottish affairs while the monarch had earlier been held in captivity for a time in England.

Albany and his sons, along with his father-in-law the Earl of Lennox were beheaded, but Dunbar and others were freed – only to be accused in 1435 of treason on what were very complex and convoluted grounds.

Although found guilty, he escaped the ultimate punishment but his lands and titles were forfeited and he spent the remainder of his life in English exile.

In September of 1650, the town of Dunbar was the scene of an infamous battle that resulted in a crushing defeat for a Scots army at the hands of England's 'Lord Protector' Oliver Cromwell and his New Model Army.

One of the most significant battles of the Third English Civil War of 1649 to 1651, it was fought between Cromwell's Parliamentary army and a Scottish Covenanting army commanded by the veteran soldier David Leslie.

The Scots were all but slaughtered, with some accounts stating there were more than 3,000 killed and up to 10,000 taken prisoner – many later transported as slaves to the colonies.

Dunbar Castle, meanwhile, in ruins since about 1567, was the original seat of the Dunbars – but that honour is now held by Mochrum Castle, Wigtownshire, in the southwest of Scotland.

Built on lands granted by King David II to Patrick Dunbar, Earl of March, Mochrum Castle is in effect two castles – a fifteenth century keep and a sixteenth century tower house.

Passed to the MacDowell Earls of Dumfries in 1694, it was bought by the Stewart Marquises of Bute in 1876 and remains in their possession to this day – but is nevertheless recognised as the Dunbar family seat.

In 1990, after lengthy consideration by the Lord Lyon King of Arms of Scotland – responsible for adjudicating on matters of genealogy and heraldry

– the Supreme Court in Edinburgh and the House of Lords, the Chiefship of Clan Dunbar was formally established.

Sir Jean Ivor Dunbar was accordingly recognised as 13th Baronet of Mochrum and Hereditary Chief of the Name and Arms of Dunbar, while on his death in 1993 the title fell to his son, as 14th Baronet, Sir James Michael Dunbar, a retired United States Air Force (USAF) colonel.

In addition to the Dunbars of Mochrum and Dunbar, meanwhile, other branches include the Dunbars of Northfield and the Dunbars of Hempriggs.

One of the most famous – although some would argue 'infamous' as a more apt description – sons of the Mochrum branch of the Dunbars was Gavin Dunbar of Mochrum.

Born in about 1490 at Mochrum, family influence came into play in 1518 when his uncle, also named Gavin Dunbar, resigned from his post of Dean of Moray and arranged for his ambitious nephew to succeed him in the post.

In 1524 he was appointed Archbishop of Glasgow, and exempted from the primary jurisdiction of the Archbishopric of St Andrews – this did not prevent the volatile Dunbar, however, from launching a physical attack on David Beaton, Archbishop of St Andrews, in 1543.

As the spirit of religious reformation had begun to take root in Scotland, Dunbar had been zealous in the persecution of those Protestant Reformers who challenged the supremacy and authority of the Roman Catholic Church.

At St Andrews in 1528, he attended the trial for heresy of the early Protestant Reformer Patrick Hamilton and was one of those who passed the death sentence on him.

Born in Linlithgow in 1504, the charismatic Hamilton was sentenced to be burnt at the stake and, accordingly, turned over to the secular authorities for the dire sentence to be carried out.

But the faggots – bundles of wood for fuel for his funeral pyre – were wet, and Hamilton, subsequently recognised as a Protestant martyr, suffered a long and agonising death.

The spot where he met his terrible fate is marked today by his monogrammed initials on cobblestones in the town's North Street, opposite St Salvator's Chapel, and to this day St Andrews University students avoid stepping on the spot because of the superstition that if they do so, they will be cursed and fail their final examinations.

Gavin Dunbar of Mochrum died in 1547, while he is also remembered for a curse he placed on the lawless Border Reivers – or raiders – in 1525.

Known as a 'Monition', it damned the reivers to hell and back by cursing everything about them to anyone who dared to aid and abet them in their nefarious activities.

Part of the curse, translated from its original Old Scots, reads:

*'I curse their head and all the hairs of their head. I curse their face, their eyes, their neck, their shoulders, their mouth, their nose, their tongue, their teeth ...*

*'I curse them going and I curse them riding. I curse them standing, and I curse them sitting. I curse them eating. I curse them drinking ...'*

*Chapter four:*
# On the world stage

**From the stage and music to literature, art and the sciences, bearers of the Dunbar name have gained distinction through a colourful variety of pursuits.**

On the stage, **Adrian Dunbar** is the Northern Irish actor born in 1958 in Enniskillen, Co. Fermanagh.

Having studied at the Guildhall School of Music and Drama, London, he has since accrued major acting credits in television, film and theatre.

Known for his role since 2012 as Superintendent Ted Hastings in the television crime thriller *Line of Duty*, his other small screen credits include *The Hollow Crown*, *Ashes to Ashes* and *The Jump*, while he was nominated for a BAFTA award for Best Original Screenplay for the 1991 film *Hear My Song*, which he wrote and in which he also starred.

Other film credits include the 1992 *The Crying Game* and, from 1989, *My Left Foot*, while numerous theatre credits include *The Exiles*, at Dublin's Abbey Theatre, and a Royal Shakespeare Company production of *The Danton Affair*.

A Scottish comedian, actress and writer, **Karen Dunbar** was born in the west coast town of Ayr in 1971 and raised in Glasgow.

A karaoke host and DJ before her talents were spotted by BBC Scotland, her television credits include the 1999 to 2002 comedy series *Chewin' the Fat* and, from 2003 to 2006, *The Karen Dunbar Show*.

In addition to a number of pantomime roles, she performed on stage in the poetic monologue *A Drunk Woman Looks at the Thistle*, while she also has a cameo role in the 2018 film *Mary, Queen of Scots*.

She featured in 2014 in the *Scotsman* newspaper's 'Pink List' of LGBT people contributing to Scotland's cultural life, while in 2015 she was awarded the Role Model of the Year Award at the Iconic Awards which celebrate the nation's LGBT community.

Going back in time, **David Dunbar** was the Australian actor of the silent film era and the early years of the 'talkies', born in 1886 in Maitland, New South Wales.

A leading actor in silent films and particularly associated with Westerns, his credits from the era of sound include the 1924 *Leatherstocking* and, from 1927, *The Arizona Whirlwind*; he died in 1953.

Still in the silent era and the early years of sound, **Dorothy Dunbar** was the American actress and socialite born in 1902 in Cripple Creek, Colorado.

Performing on stage as a child actor, it was after being attracted by the bright lights of Hollywood that she was signed up to a film contract in 1924 and, two years later, starred in *The Amateur Gentleman*.

Also starring in the 1927 *Tarzan and the Golden Lion*, she became the fourth actress to take on the role of Jane.

Married seven times, including to the South American millionaire Jaime De Garson, the boxer and actor Max Baer and the portrait painter Tino Costa, she died in 1992.

From the stage to literature and travelling back through the dim mists of time to mid-fifteenth and early sixteenth century Scotland, **William Dunbar** was the poet – also known in Scots as a makar – whose most notable works were composed while serving at the court of King James IV.

Born in about 1459 in East Lothian, he was employed in royal duties after studying at St Andrews University and also serving abroad for a time on a number of diplomatic missions.

Composing verse on a wide and colourful range of subjects, one of his best known works is the allegory *The Thrissil and the Rose* (*The Thistle and the Rose*), commemorating the marriage in 1503 of King James IV to Margaret of England.

He died in about 1530, while he is commemorated through Makar's Court, outside the Writers' Museum in Edinburgh's Lawnmarket area.

In much later times, **Paul Laurence Dunbar** was the poet, playwright and novelist recognised as 'one of the first African-American writers to establish an international reputation.'

Born in 1872 in Dayton, Ohio, to parents who had been slaves, his first poems were published in a local newspaper when he was aged only 16, setting him on the path to a prolific poetic output.

He also penned the lyrics for the 1903 musical comedy *Dahomey* – the first all African-American musical to be produced on Broadway and which later also toured the rest of the United States and the United Kingdom.

He died from tuberculosis in 1906, at the age of only 33, in his home town of Dayton.

From literature to the equally creative world of art, **John Dunbar** is the British artist, collector and former gallery owner closely associated with the pop culture of the 1960s.

Born in Mexico City in 1942, his father was the film producer, director and writer **Robert Dunbar**, born in 1914 and who died in 2000, and mother Tatiana, the daughter of Russian émigrés.

He married the singer Marianne Faithfull in 1965 but divorced five years later, while in the same year of his marriage he also co-founded the Indica Gallery, in London.

Famed for staging exhibitions of the work of avant-garde artists, it was here that he famously introduced John Lennon to Yoko Ono.

Bearers of the Dunbar name have gained recognition in the world of the sciences.

An American astronomer and planetologist, **Roy Scott Dunbar** has been instrumental in the discovery of a number of minor planets and comets.

The co-discoverer from 1981 to 1987 of ten minor planets, it was along with Maria A. Baruci that he discovered the Aten asteroid *3551 Verenia* and, with Eleanor Helin, minor planets including *3360 Syrinx* and *6435 Daveross*.

The main-belt asteroid *3718 Dunbar* was

named in his honour in 1988 after being discovered by Eleanor Helin and Schelte Bus.

Also taking to the heavens, **Bonnie Jeanne Dunbar** is the former astronaut who, after retiring from NASA in 2005, served as president of America's Museum of Flight, Seattle, for a time before heading the University of Houston's STEM (Science, Technology, Engineering and Mathematics) Center.

Born in 1949 in Sunnyside, Washington, she has also held the post of professor of engineering at Texas A and M University.

From space to natural history, **Carl Owen Dunbar** was the American palaeontologist whose textbook series on historical geology, published from the 1920s to the 1950s, has sold in excess of one million copies.

Born in 1891 in Hallowell, Cherokee County, Kansas, and specialising in invertebrate fossils, before his death in 1979 he was the recipient of many prestigious honours that include election to the U.S. National Academy of Sciences and the Paleontological Medal.

Born in Edinburgh in 1918, **Isobel Dunbar** was the Scots-Canadian glaciologist and Arctic ice researcher who was the first woman to conduct scientific research from Canadian icebreaker vessels and among the first women to fly over the North Pole.

A Fellow of the Royal Society of Canada, Officer of the Order of Canada and recipient of the Royal Canadian Geographical Society's Massey Medal "for her excellent work in arctic geography and sea ice", she died in 1999.

From science to music, **Ronald Dunbar** was the American songwriter, record producer and A. and R. (Artists and Repertoire) director born in 1939 in Detroit, Michigan.

Frequently working in close collaboration with the equally legendary song writing team Holland-Dozier-Holland (Brian Holland, Lamont Dozier and Eddie Holland, Jr.), he was responsible before his death in 2018 for a number of classic hits including Freda Payne's *Band of Gold*, *Give Me Just a Little More Time*, by Chairmen of the Board and Clarence Carter's *Patches*, for which he won the 1971 Grammy Award for Best R. and B. Song.

Behind the drum kit, **Aynsley Dunbar** is the veteran rock drummer born in Liverpool in 1946.

Much in demand and an inductee of the Rock and Roll Hall of Fame in 2017 as drummer with the band Journey, other artists he has played for include

Frank Zappa, Jefferson Starship, David Bowie and Keith Emerson.

From music to the highly competitive world of sport, one American tennis player with two rather unusual claims to fame is **Vicki-Nelson Dunbar**.

Born in 1962, at the time of writing she holds the record for playing in the longest-ever women's tennis match.

This was in September of 1984 at a tournament in Richmond, Virginia, against Jean Hepner – the hotly-contested encounter lasting 6 hours and 31 minutes.

The match also set a record for the longest rally in tennis history – a 643-shot rally that lasted 29 minutes.

# Greek Island Myths

# RHODES
## THE COLOSSUS

JILL DUDLEY

PUT IT IN YOUR POCKET SERIES
ORPINGTON PUBLISHERS

*Published by*
Orpington Publishers

*Cover design and origination by*
Creeds, Bridport, Dorset
01308 423411

*Printed and bound in the UK by*
Creeds

© Jill Dudley 2016

ISBN: 978-0-9935378-0-6

# RHODES

## THE COLOSSUS

Rhodes is the largest of the Dodecanese islands in the Aegean. It is an island of sea, sunshine and flowers; an island of ancient and medieval history; of glorious temples to the gods, and great buildings left by the Knights of St. John of Jerusalem.

Legend has it that in antiquity Zeus, supreme god of the Olympians and god of the heavens, when dividing up the earth amongst his family, overlooked the sun-god Helios. On finding he had been forgotten, Helios complained to Zeus who immediately awarded him an island which had just emerged out of the deep; this was the beautiful, flower-bedecked island of Rhodes.

In those ancient times Helios had been regarded as a charioteer with a team of four fiery horses who drew him across the heavens daily from east to west heralded by Eos (the dawn). At night it was said he disappeared to the other side of the earth in a golden bowl floating on Ocean, the sea that girdled the globe.

The story goes that Helios married Rhodos (daughter of Poseidon, god of the sea), hence the name of the island. The first cities, founded in the second millennium B.C., were named after three of Helios' grandsons: Lindos, Ialyssos and Kameiros. The city of Rhodes on the northern tip of the island was founded later in 408 B.C. Where the imposing Crusader Palace of the Grand Masters stands today there was once a great temple of Helios, no doubt with a view over the city to the sea and the rising sun in the east.

It was at Mandraki harbour in Rhodes city that the famous Colossus stood. The Colossus was a gigantic bronze statue of Helios, one hundred and fourteen feet high, weighing twenty tons. It was cast by Chares of Lindos in 280 B.C. and took twelve years to complete. In fact it was left to one of his pupils to finish because Chares discovered he had made some fearful blunder in his calculations and, rather than face the disgrace of being thought incompetent, committed suicide. With its completion, it was lifted up to stand, not astride the harbour mouth – that was a misconception spread about in the Middle Ages – but on a pedestal to one side of the harbour. The fingers alone on the Colossus were each the size of a man and, due to its immense size, it became one of the seven wonders of the world. The enormous head was surrounded by sun-rays.

The Colossus was built in celebration of the island's triumphant defeat of Cyprus. Some say Cyprus attacked the city for a whole year using a gargantuan bronze siege-machine which the Rhodians finally managed to overturn by tunnelling under it. At all events, the enemy sailed away leaving their weapons, and the Colossus was forged with the metal from the arsenal they left behind.

But this wonder of the world, this statue of Helios the sun-god, was not destined to overlook the harbour entrance for long. Seventy years after it was erected, a great earthquake caused it to crack at the knees and it came crashing down, and broke into pieces.

In time the worship of Helios in Rhodes was taken over by Apollo who became equated with the sun – Phoebus Apollo as he was commonly known, meaning Apollo the shining one, Apollo, god of light. On the upper acropolis of Rhodes city are the few remaining columns of the ancient temple of Apollo Pythia (the epithet Pythia comes from Apollo's priestess at Delphi, the spokeswoman for Apollo). From this high elevation, there is a distant view over the rooftops of the city's buildings to the glittering sapphire-blue sea where majestic white cruise liners sail into harbour. No doubt their passengers, standing on deck and looking towards the island, can see the few soaring columns of Apollo's temple rising against the skyline.

From the terrace of the temple of Apollo, the ground descends steeply to a lower terrace to a stadium where once the Alioi Games were held. These were part of a major festival held in honour of Helios. To one side of the stadium is a small theatre whose tiered seats are of white marble. It was used not so much for drama as a venue for classes in oratory and rhetoric for which Rhodes became famous. The great Roman orator Cicero was said to have spent time in this theatre where he was taught to curb his impetuous and exuberant nature. Julius Caesar had also come here when, as a young man, he had felt the need to perfect his oratory, realizing that it was his most powerful weapon for swaying public opinion.

The whole vast temple complex – and there are temples there also of Zeus and Athena – was created for the citizens of Rhodes as a sacred area for religious, educational and recreational purposes. Everywhere the deep blue-green of juniper trees with their spreading branches offer welcome shade. It is a unique location with a therapeutic feel to it.

Lindos, the capital before the foundation of Rhodes town, remained the religious centre of the island. On its great rocky promontory overlooking the sea are the remains of the ancient temple of Athena dating from around 300 B.C., though the goddess was worshipped there as early as the tenth century B.C.

It is said that Rhodes island sent nine ships to the Trojan War. Two marble plaques have been found on the site, one listing the priests who served the goddess, and the other inscribed with both her miracles and the names of eminent people who once visited her temple. Amongst those mentioned were Helen of Troy* and her husband King Menelaus; this must have been after the downfall of Troy when Menelaus was reconciled with his wife Helen, the most beautiful woman in the world – reconciled because, of course, she had been seduced by Paris, the King of Troy's son.

The beauty of Rhodes lies in its sunshine and light which intensify the colours of the sea from shades of sapphire-blue, to aquamarine, to turquoise, to a whitish-blue; the sea and sky contrast with the brilliant shades of its forest greens: emerald, bottle- and blue-green.

Sunshine! There is nothing more dependable than the sun rising at dawn and setting at dusk. In Greek myth, however, there was one occasion when Helios failed and calamity struck. The story is that one day Helios as a kindly father rashly promised Phaethon (his son) that he would grant whatever he most wished for. Having watched his father handle his chariot and horses daily, Phaethon asked to be allowed to take the reins and do it on his own. Despite Helios' concern and doubts as to his son's ability to control the horses, as he had given his promise he felt obliged to allow him, and so handed over the reins to Phaethon. The result was just as Helios had feared; his son did not have the strength to stop the horses from bolting. They first galloped up to the heavens, leaving a path which some say became the Milky Way; then they charged earthwards, scorching the world and turning all people near the equator black. Lord Zeus, seeing catastrophe looming, threw a thunderbolt and poor Phaethon fell in flames to his death. His sisters, who had been watching the whole sorry spectacle, wept inconsolably until the gods took pity and turned them into poplars, and their tears were hardened by Helios and turned to amber.

Fortunately, no lasting damage was done to the horses and chariot, and so Helios returned to his duty. Today few people think of, or even know the story. They go to Rhodes for the sunshine and the sea. They go for its historic past too, but few look at the sky and think to themselves there goes Helios in his chariot drawn by his four fiery horses.

Sometimes the modern age loses out on imaginative ideas. Scientific facts have taken over which cut out the fanciful myths of the past. It is a great pity, though luckily the stories are never quite forgotten.

*\* Denotes a separate booklet on the subject.*

# FAMILY TREE OF HELIOS AND ATHENA

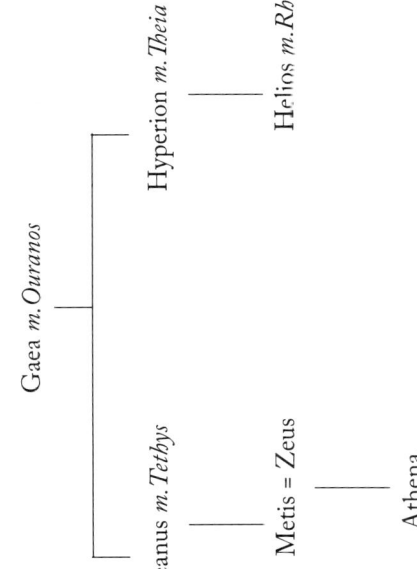

# GLOSSARY OF GODS AND GODDESSES

APOLLO – Son of Zeus and Leto, and twin brother of Artemis. He was god of music, archery and prophecy.

ATHENA – Daughter of Zeus. She was born mature and fully armed from his head. She was goddess of victory, and patroness of handicraft and, as Athena Polias, was protectress of cities. She was also regarded as the embodiment of wisdom.

HELIOS – A Greek sun-god, and a Titan. He married Rhodos.

PHAETHON – Son of Helios and Clymene, a sea-nymph.

POSEIDON – Brother of Zeus. He was god of the sea as well as of earthquakes and horses.

RHODOS – Wife of Helios, and daughter of Poseidon and Amphitrite, after whom the island of Rhodes was named.

ZEUS – Supreme god of the ancient world, god of the heavens who was often referred to as the 'cloud-gatherer'. He was protector of law and justice.

MORE FROM THE
PUT IT IN YOUR POCKET SERIES
## GREEK MYTHS

### TROJAN WAR
THE JUDGEMENT OF PARIS
HELEN
KING AGAMEMNON
ACHILLES
THE WOODEN HORSE
ODYSSEUS

### SACRED SITES
ATHENS – THE ACROPOLIS
CORINTH – ST. PAUL AND THE GODDESS OF LOVE
DELPHI – THE ORACLE OF APOLLO
ELEUSIS – DEMETER AND KORE
EPIDAURUS – CENTRE OF HEALING
OLYMPIA – THE OLYMPIC GAMES

ALSO BY JILL DUDLEY

YE GODS! (TRAVELS IN GREECE)

YE GODS! II (MORE TRAVELS IN GREECE)

LAP OF THE GODS (TRAVELS IN CRETE
AND THE AEGEAN ISLANDS)